Goal Driven Evangelism

J Daniel Barnes

Table of Contents

Worksheets

Introduction

Evangelism can be a frightening thing. Few things get the heart pounding of the average "Sunday-Morning-go-to-Meetin' Christian" like the thought of talking to people about Jesus. We all know we need to share our faith with the world, but telling others about what we believe can seem scary and overwhelming. Religion often causes disagreement and confrontation, and that can be tense. Everyone has heard the old rule: "Never discuss politics or religion in social situations." We are not equipped, don't know what to say, and are unable to answer hard questions. We feel ignorant when confronted by an individual of another religion; it can be frightening. In addition, we have so much to do and so little time to do it. All these reasons, and more, are often given share; but, the reason to share is even more compelling. A mandate is given from our Lord Jesus Christ. The Great Commission commands us to go. Jesus gave the command and He provides the tools. He won't leave us on our own. Our Lord did not equip us for failure.

Jesus came and told his disciples, "I have been given complete authority in heaven and on earth. Therefore, go and make disciples of all the nations, baptizing them in the name of the Father and the Son and the Holy Spirit. Teach these new disciples to obey all the commands I have given you. And be sure of this: I am with you always, even to the end of the age." Matthew 28:18-20

Obeying fear is disobeying our responsibility from Christ. He issued a command and included the promise that He will be with us until the end of time. And yet, we struggle and fight against our clear duty. We know we should share the gospel, and deep down we have the desire, but we still struggle. If you didn't believe in sharing Jesus with others, you wouldn't be reading this book. We all struggle with effectively sharing our faith from time to time. What we need is the proper mindset.

Evangelism doesn't begin with a tool, a strategy, or a plan. Evangelism begins with a change in your life. You find the Living Water and desire to share it. We all desire to share Jesus, but so much gets in the way. We often believe we don't know enough; or maybe we know too much but don't know how to share. All these things are secondary to desiring a knowledge of Christ. That's where we must begin the process that leads us to share what we believe with anyone.

In the following pages are tools to use as you begin sharing you faith; tools that will guide you when talking to those around you about the most important aspect of your life. Everyone has certain people who they see, contact, or share life with every day. These people are in our social circle; we influence them and they influence us. We help these people, give them advice, share ideas, and discuss decisions. But too often, we are silent about the most important decision in their lives. Within these pages you will find a way to share what you believe with those in your circle, and you will learn to share in a way that is conversational, comfortable, and enjoyable. As you share it will become easier. The Holy Spirit is true to His word. He will give you the words to speak and the boldness to speak them. I am excited that you chose this journey with me, and I trust we will learn much together. I hope you enjoy this material as much as I enjoyed seeing it unfold.

Dan

The Theology of Evangelism

Don't turn back now by letting the word "theology" freak you out. Theology means the study of God and the things of God. It's important to understand what God has called us to do regarding Evangelism. We are here on earth as the ambassadors of Christ, left to preach and teach and make disciples. We must examine the mission of Jesus, the instructions He gave to His followers, and then follow in their footsteps. Don't be overwhelmed with guilt and shame. You can do this. It's easier than you think; you just have to get started.

Jesus came telling people to repent from sin. "Repent" means turning away and fleeing from something; to simply turn tail and run. The command is simple: follow God by trusting in Jesus and living by faith. On a couple of different occasions, Jesus sent His followers out to share. In Matthew 10, He sent the twelve disciples to proclaim "the Kingdom of Heaven is at hand" and to heal the sick, raise the dead, and cast out demons. They went from town to town doing this, and proclaiming to all Israel that hope had arrived. The people of Israel would understand. The Jews were waiting for the Messiah, the anointed one. Jesus had come and the disciples spread the news that Jesus had come to save them.

The second time, Jesus sends out 72 of His followers into towns preceding His visit. The message was the same: "The Kingdom of God has come near to you", meaning that the Messiah (or, Christ in Greek), the one sent by God to save the people, had arrived. He was coming to their town and they needed to be ready. The promised Savior had come.

After the death, burial, and resurrection of Jesus, He sent out His followers again, but this time their mission was permanent. This is "The Great Commission", and it's important for all of us to understand.

"Jesus came and told his disciples, 'I have been given all authority in heaven and on earth. Therefore, go and make disciples of all the nations, baptizing them in the name of the Father and the Son and the Holy Spirit. Teach these new disciples to obey all the commands I have given you. And be sure of this: I am with you always, even to the end of the age'." Matthew 28:18-20.

The command to go given by Jesus could be translated "while you are on your way", or "as you go". Jesus basically said to bear witness of His salvation and make disciples as you go through life. He did not call us to quit our jobs, sell everything, and move to the international mission field. God calls some to that specific work, but for others it's simple. Go to work, go to school, go to the store, and go about your life. And as you go these places, talk about your faith, share it with others, tell them the Good News, and pray for them.

The reality about sharing our faith is this: if we don't, who will? If you knew something that would save someone's life, would you tell them? If the building you were in caught fire, would you sound the alarm? If you could save someone from death, would you? Most would say "of course", but talking about Salvation is difficult for many. We don't think often about death or the people around us dying. We seldom stop to consider what would happen if those people died. It's easy to just assume everyone will be fine and all will end up in Heaven. Sadly, this isn't the case. Jesus said, "You can enter God's Kingdom only through the narrow gate. The highway to hell is broad, and its gate is wide for the many who choose that way." (Matthew 7:13). In verse 14, He continues, "But the gateway to life is very narrow and the road is difficult, and only a few ever find it." It is hard to accept that many people are going to hell because of their choices; because the hardness of their hearts make them unwilling to turn to Christ.

The fact that few find the path to Salvation shouldn't keep us from sharing, it should encourage us to share all the more. We don't want to be the reason someone missed Heaven. Sometimes the difference between eternity in paradise or an eternity of torment is a few words from a friend. Giving someone hope, sharing love, and reaching out can make a giant difference. The theology of Evangelism is simple; summed up in John 3:16, that God loves the world of humanity and sent Jesus to save it. Jesus has returned to the Father, and now it's our job to bring His hope to the world. We must have love and compassion for the world, to see it like Jesus did. Evangelism isn't about packing out an area, having a bunch of people at church, winning a prize, or being noticed and esteemed. It's about love and compassion for the world that is trapped in sin, mired in selfishness, prisoners to unrighteousness, and needing help getting out. They need Jesus, and we have the opportunity to share with them. As you go, will you share what God has given you?

The Mindset of Evangelism

Before any planning or strategy is outlined, we must first address our mindset, our way of thinking. The things we do, and the actions we take, all start with an idea and a plan. We begin with a desire to get it done, and then we take action. We must get our minds ready for action. To share the Gospel the way Jesus desires, we must see people the way Jesus saw them. This statement He made shows how Jesus feels:

"O Jerusalem, Jerusalem, the city that kills the prophets and stones God's messengers! How often I have wanted to gather your children together as a hen protects her chicks beneath her wings, but you wouldn't let me." Matthew 23:37

The city that would soon mob Him and cry, "Crucify Him!" was this very city over which Jesus wept. His compassion for the lost is demonstrated several times when He looks at the crowd (see Matthew 9:36, 14:14, 15:32, and 20:34). He calls us to have the same compassion for the lost. Such compassion is shown by a broken heart burdened with the knowledge that many are headed for a place the Bible calls Hell. A desire to share the love of Jesus and a compassion for lost people is the beginning of sharing. We should stand and look at our city and be moved with compassion for those who are lost like sheep without a shepherd. We must realize that people apart from Christ are trapped by their sin. They are in slavery to sin and fleshly desires, and they need a Savior to free them.

Many of us can share where we are; our job, school, or even our home. Perhaps our friends or some social organization of which we are a part provides opportunities. The places we frequent and invest ourselves can be the best places to look for opportunities. Look around for the lost you come in contact with daily. Keep your eyes and heart open, and follow the leading of the Holy Spirit.

The first obstacle we must overcome is our existing mindset. We must exchange if for the mindset of Christ.

Don't copy the behavior and customs of this world, but let God transform you into a new person by changing the way you think. Then you will learn to know God's will for you, which is good and pleasing and perfect. Romans 12:2

Our thinking regarding reaching out and sharing our faith must be transformed. Each of us struggle with selfishness that comes with this world. It's easier to look out for ourselves and not have compassion toward others. We need to change our outlook on life and the way we look at the world. How is God calling you to change your outlook in regard to Evangelism?

It's important to evaluate how we look at people. When you meet someone for the first time, what comes to mind? Do you evaluate their physical appearance? Maybe you notice their clothes or haircut? Perhaps you notice if they are shy or outgoing, look for a good personality, a sense of humor, or some other trait. Can you read a person on first meeting them? Maybe you find yourself drawn to people who are most like you. It's human nature to surround yourself with people with whom you share an interest. Do you live out the idea that "birds of a feather flock together", or are you more of an "opposites attract" sort of person? Each of us value different traits. We each see different things when we look at people. How does the Holy Spirit relate to people? What did Jesus see when He looked at people?

Read Matthew 8:1-4. In Jesus' day, a person with a communicable skin condition was required to live outside the camp or city. These diseases were fungal and could be spread from person to person with simple contact. Persons so afflicted were required to publicly proclaim themselves "unclean" when people approached too closely. They were looked down on, considered outcast by society, and had to live outside the city walls.

As Christians we sometimes look with judgmental eyes at the world. We look at those trapped in the prison and disease of sin and consider them "unclean". Things seem to be getting worse all the time. We have forgotten what sin is and what it has done to this world. Jesus knew what sin was and out of compassion He paid the price for it. We are unable to save people from sin; all we must do is tell them how to become free. Christians have been set free and are no longer called sinners, but saints. We still struggle with sin, but for those who are born again, it's not a prison. Sin is a prison for those who have not accepted Christ. A sinful man cannot live a Godly life. We must have compassion. We cannot expect a non-Christian to have Christian morals or a Christ-like attitude. There are many self-confessed "good people" in the world, but they all suffer from the same terminal disease of sin. They are trapped and need our help.

Successful evangelism flows from compassion for the lost world. Many of us have compassion but are afraid to speak and unsure of what to say. Sometimes we look at the world that rebels against God and lose our compassion. This is the same issue many of the Old Testament prophets faced. The God they served is the same God we serve today, and we can see how He provided for them. They were human, they struggled with speaking, sharing, and sometimes they lost their compassion; yet, God used them in amazing ways. God empowered them, and we serve that same God today. Let's looks at some of the promises He made to men of the Old Testament.

Moses. "Now go, and do as I have told you. I will help you speak well, and I will tell you what to say." Exodus 4:12

Isaiah. "And I have put my words in your mouth and hidden you safely within my hand. I set all the stars in space and established the earth. I am the one who says to Israel, `You are mine!" Isaiah 51:16

"It is the same with my word. I send it out, and it always produces fruit. It will accomplish all I want it to, and it will prosper everywhere I send it." Isaiah 55:11

Jeremiah. "Don't say that," the LORD replied, "for you must go wherever I send you and say whatever I tell you. And don't be afraid of the people, for I will be with you and take care of you. I, the LORD, have spoken!" Then the LORD touched my mouth and said, "See, I have put my words in your mouth! Today I appoint you to stand up against nations and kingdoms. You are to uproot some and tear them down, to destroy and overthrow them. You are to build others up and plant them." Jeremiah 1:7-10

In the Great Commission, Jesus gave us the same promise: He will be with us until the very end. God the Father and God the Son have both promised to guide us in our efforts. There are two critical aspects to sharing your faith; the heart of compassion, and the Spirit of God. The words and phrases that come next are easy, and can be taught and learned. A heart for God and compassion like Jesus is something no one can teach you. It is given by the Lord.

Many of us never consider the spiritual condition of those around us. Even those of us involved in evangelism programs at our church only think about sharing during that hour or two a week. In the middle of our busy schedules we seldom think about sharing the Gospel with the lost. We often forget how our friends and co-workers stand in relation to the Kingdom of Heaven. So much of our life is compartmentalized. We ensure everything has its proper place. We have the mindset that there is a time for talking about God, and a time not to talk about God. It's acceptable for us to talk about God on Sunday, but we seldom think about it on Monday morning. We must move beyond this compartmentalized mindset and introduced evangelism into our everyday life.

It is my hope and prayer that your heart will be filled with ciompassion toward everyone you meet, and the first thing you look for is their knowledge of the Lord. I encourage you to ask the Lord each time you meet someone how you should share the Gospel. This is the mind and heart of Christ. He came to set the captives free, and calls us to be involved in His work. It should be our first priority, that thing which drives us in our daily lives. It should give you motivation to be among lost people, talking and sharing with people at work, at school, or in social situations. Evangelism must be on our hearts and minds at all times.

What type of Evangelist are you?

Many Christians avoid sharing their faith by claiming it's not their gift. If you read Ephesians 4:11, you'll see a list of roles for God's people, of which Evangelists are a part. Many Christians, who do not share their faith, say they do not have the gift or role of evangelism. Many of us do not have this gift, but each of us are called to be Great Commission-fulfilling Christians. The difference between these two is in the audience. Billy Graham is the best example of an evangelist. He shares the Gospel successfully as his lifelong ministry with large groups. We will use the word Evangelist in this study, but we are actually referring to a Great Commission Christian, one who shares his or her faith with others. This usually doesn't involve large rallies or mass presentations (if God is leading you this direction, then follow His lead). We will speak of an evangelist as anyone who shares his or her faith in any situation. We are examining sharing our faith in a personal one-on-one context, to which everyone is called and anyone can do.

The first step in sharing the Gospel is understanding who you are. We are all created unique and different, and our interactions with people are always different. Each of us must understand who we are before trying to share with someone else. It is important to know what kind of evangelist you are. We all have gifts, and we must learn how to use our gifts to share our faith. If your gift is teaching, or singing, or administration, God can use that gift to tell others about Jesus. Each of us have a unique role to fill in the Body of Christ, and in doing so, we each have unique opportunities. We also have different personality types, and each personality will share somewhat differently.

Here are some questions to get you thinking:

Circle the word or phrase that best fits you.

-In a social situation, are you shy or outgoing?

-Do you make new friends quickly and easily or slowly get to know people?

-Do you enjoy going out or staying in?

-How do you feel about public speaking, eager or hesitant?

-How well do you handle confrontation? Do you confront or ignore?

-When a task is given, do you lead, or follow?

-Do you embrace or avoid confrontation?

Now that we are beginning to think about our personalities, let's look at the different Evangelist types. Each of us will generally fit into one of three categories in relation to sharing our faith. These coincide with our personalities and the gifts and talents God has given us. Are you Active, Passive, or Not Me?

-Active Evangelist. Are you outgoing? Do you make friends quickly? Do you long for the spotlight and enjoy crowds? Have you ever sat and talked with a missionary from a cult, or a member of a different religion? Perhaps you're an active evangelist. An active evangelist doesn't shy away from talking with people, even about controversial subjects such as abortion, gay marriage, and Christianity. An Active Evangelist wants to be in the middle of the conversation and the controversy. If this sounds like you, you may have experienced the following roadblocks:

-Arguments about religion.

-Confrontation and/or overwhelming the person to whom you are talking.

-People making commitments as lip service only, and never following though.

Most active evangelists have strong personalities that often draw people to them. This is a great characteristic, but can result in people accepting you and not Jesus. This will not cause life-change or commitment. It is important to use the proper tools and be sure you are sharing clearly and in a way that leads to Christ.

An Active Evangelist may sound like this:

"I really enjoy my biology class, I look forward to it every day. My professor and I constantly debate topics like evolution and creation. I've done a great deal of research, and today I have some great points to make."

"Every year over the summer, we make a trip to visit the LDS Temple in Salt Lake City to hand out tracts and talk to LDS people. I always invite Mormon Missionaries in to talk and debate with them. Sometimes we get into arguments and they leave mad, but I think it's because I made a good point."

Passive Evangelist. Do you try to share your faith, but are naturally reclusive? Do you try to witness in less confrontational ways? Do you leave tracts on the table at a restaurant with your tip? Do you wear Christian T-shirts? Do agree to disagree with cult members? Have you ever turned all the radio stations on display radios in a store to a Christian station? You may be a passive Evangelist. As a passive Evangelist, you may have experienced the following problems:

-Shying away before inviting someone to receive Christ.

-Not sharing the full gospel because the other person changed the subject.

-Not being able to express what you believe or are trying to say.

-Not being sure of what to say if someone asks a question.

As a passive evangelist, the hardest obstacle is overcoming your sense of dread regarding sharing the Gospel. The process becomes easier as you find a strategy that works for you and begin building redemptive relationships. Don't give up. Press on, and remember in all things, pray.

A Passive Evangelist may sound like this:

"I always keep tracts in my pocket, so I can leave them on the table in a restaurant or in other public places. I try to be nice to people, and wear a Christian t-shirt, and I pray they will see my witness and get saved."

"I always invite my friends to church. I think it's the best way for them to hear about Jesus. I try to talk about it, but I just don't know what to say."

-Not Me Evangelist. When you hear the word evangelism, does your heart beat uncontrollably? Perhaps you wish you could share your faith, but the thought is terrifying. Have you ever been in a situation where you wanted to share your faith, but were just too afraid? Are you hesitant to wear a Christian T-shirt or other symbol because you don't want people asking you questions? You are probably a "Not Me" Evangelist. You may have experienced problems like:

-Being unsure of what to say when trying to witness.

-Nervousness and fear that keeps you from saying anything.

-Avoiding situations in which you would be asked to speak or share your testimony.

-Avoiding relationships with outgoing Christians.

As a "Not Me" Evangelist, you have taken a big step by coming this far. Picking up a resource about sharing your faith may be a little daunting. It is my prayer that you will continue searching for a way to share your faith and be successful. I promise not to heap guilt upon you or pressure you as a "Not Me" Evangelist: but I urge and encourage you to both consider and try to apply these principles.

A "Not Me" Evangelist may sound like this:

"Our church was having an outreach day, and people went to knock on doors and ask some questions and share about Jesus. I just about fainted even thinking about doing something like that."

"I had my Bible in my briefcase one day, and a co-worker asked me about it. I told him where I go to church. He looked like he was waiting for me to say something else, but I didn't know what to say. Finally he left and I was so relieved. I couldn't imagine talking about church with the people at work; I wouldn't know what to say."

Many of us fit in between the categories. Perhaps you are part "not me" and part passive, or in between passive and active. It is not my goal to place you in a neat category, but help you discover more about you. As we learn about ourselves we can overcome the problems limiting us and move closer to being a powerful and effective witness for Jesus Christ. We are all individuals with different skills and talents, but the Lord wants to use each of those in our lives. The key is to not try to change yourself. You don't have to become someone different to share your faith. God wants to use you where you are. He has given you the tools you need and will be with you as you use them. Just be who He is shaping you into being, and share your faith where you are.

Personalities of the Lost

Just like we each have different personalities, each person we encounter is also a little different. Everyone has a background and personality type that makes them unique. I have found five different categories into which people generally fit. Some fall into two categories and overlap slightly, but everyone should fit into one of these categories. Each group has its own obstacles to overcome with plans and strategies that are helpful for each. The most successful plan is relationship-building. It is vital to build a relationship with those with whom we are sharing and help them overcome whatever keeps them from the Good News of Jesus Christ. Some of the individuals we will share with have had negative experiences with Christians or churches, so we must love them and care about them before we can share anything. Learning about the person you desire to share with is integral. Remember, they are God's creation with eternal souls. They are worth the investment of our time.

-The Opposing View. The Opposer is that person who has a belief in opposition to the claims of Jesus Christ. Muslims, Buddhists, Mormons, and others are all types of Opposers. These are the groups with whom Active Evangelists find themselves enmeshed in confrontation. They have bought into the dogma their particular church teaches. There are also Opposers in our churches who believe in untruths, such as earned (works-based) salvation. Often these people just do not understand, or have been under a teacher or pastor who was unlearned in theology. Atheists also fall into this group, although they do not believe God exists. Atheism is still very much a belief system. Opposers necessitate a great deal of time and patience when sharing God's truth. We must always share in love. An argument is never the way to help the Opposer. Most Opposers hold to their beliefs as strongly as Christians believe in Christ. There are churches in your community that bear the name Christian or Christ in name, but they are not Christian in their teachings about God, Jesus, or the Bible. Opposers are the most common group of non-Christians you will encounter, and are the most difficult ones with whom we must share. Thanks to the power of the Holy Spirit, these people can be won to the Lord, but it takes time and lots of prayer. With God, all things are possible.

-The Skeptic. The Skeptic is similar to the Opposer, but does not have a core belief system. The skeptic may see his or herself as an intellectual and declare that believing in God is outdated. They may embrace science and secular society and reject belief in God. Perhaps they are not as adamant in their rejection as an atheist. They may believe in God, but not have clear opinions about God or Jesus. We often call these people agnostic. Agnostic comes from the Greek word 'gnosis' that means belief or knowledge. Just like 'a-theist' in Greek means 'no god', 'a-gnostic' means no belief or no knowledge. An agnostic has no set of concrete beliefs. Many reject the church and belief in God based on what they have seen in others who claim to follow Christ. They may make comments like "the church is full of hypocrites". Other skeptics will believe in God, but reject Jesus or his Lordship. They may make comments such as "I don't need to go to church to believe in God". They may have had a bad experience with Christianity, or been in a group that teased Christians, and decided to reject it. Someone close to them who attended church regularly, such as a relative or family member, may have hurt them. Perhaps someone in his or her family was a deacon or a pastor, but did not live a Christ-centered lifestyle. They may ask questions such as "If there is a God, why does He allow people like this in the church?" or "If God loves us, why do all these bad things happen?" Many churches have endured painful splits and fights over things that do not seem very Godly, like tile or carpet color, worship style, or Sunday School structure. They may harbor anger toward God. A skeptic could be a casualty of wars within the church. It will take much time and unconditional love to heal these wounds.

-The Almost but Not Quite. The "Not Quiter" has been taught about Jesus. Maybe they were raised in Church or grew up in Sunday School and Vacation Bible School. They understand their personal sin and need for Jesus, but have decided against following Jesus because they want to live their lives apart from His will or desires. They are not ready or willing to live in surrender to Jesus. Many may express their intent to become a Christian in later years after their own plans are fulfilled. They are usually opposed to perceived rules regarding Christianity and reject it without serious investigation. Because of this popular misconception, they believe God is the great kill-joy and is against any type of fun.

There is another category of "Not Quiters", but altogether different. These are people who believe they are Christians, but have never committed their heart and life to Jesus Christ. Perhaps they were raised in church, have "gone through all the motions", their dad was a deacon, and mom played the organ. Possibly they are married to or dating a Christian, so they believe they are going to Heaven by default. They may sit in the same place every Sunday and believe that is adequate to get them into Heaven. These people are almost in the family of God, but not quite. They have some level of head knowledge, but lack the commitment of the heart.

-The Outsider. The Outsider doesn't know anything about Jesus. They didn't grow up going to church, they didn't spend much time with Christians, and they don't think about God. They may consider themselves spiritual, but no one has ever told them anything about Jesus. The only exposure they may have had is through movies or television. They may be disinterested when presented with the claims of Christ because of images gained from popular culture. They may or may not believe in Heaven or Hell; if they do, most will believe they are destined for Heaven because they see themselves as good people. This is most likely the limit of their spiritual knowledge. It may seem absurd to think of people in our culture who have never heard the Gospel, but they exist. Keep your eyes and ears open, and you will discover them.

-The Seeker. The seeker will often seek you out. They sense there is more to this life than what they have experienced and are searching for it. They are open to conversations about the Bible, attending a Bible Study, church service, or event. They may possess little knowledge about Jesus but are open to the truth. They ask questions and are receptive. This group is the easiest with which to share. They will come to church or your Bible study eagerly.

Many people with whom we come in contact will blend into more than one category. Everyone will be a little different, but remember that God loves each one of them as much as He loves you, and Jesus died for them just as He died for you. Keep this mindset regardless of with whom you are talking or how they respond. Everyone is worth the effort of sharing. Remember the words of Jesus: "Healthy people don't need a doctor—sick people do. I have come to call sinners, not those who think they are already good enough." Mark 2:17

Those who are in the strongest bondage to sin need to hear the gospel most of all. It may be our first instinct to write off those most resistant, those who are most obstinate; but these are often the ones with whom God is dealing the most. Something is happening inside those who react strongly against the Gospel. It can be a past hurt or a current problem. They may be fighting against the Gospel, or the notion that they could be destined for Hell. There is often more happening inside than a simple disagreement. People seldom become emotional over issues in which they have no interest. I can't recall anyone becoming upset when hearing about Santa Claus, even though he requires children to earn his toys with good behavior. People seldom get angry when talking about Buddha, or new age crystals; but the claims of Christ often stir intense emotions. Pay attention to hurt feelings and past hurts and disappointments. These can be just the openings you need to share the truth in love. Remember, above all things, pray.

Entry Points

An entry point is the place where you begin your gospel presentation. Every entry point is different. Some begin journeys last a long time. Others lead into a Gospel presentation resulting in the person committing themselves to Christ in a short time. This first step must be taken with great care, but seems innocuous. All entry points begin with a simple conversation or question. I recently began a conversation with a student by asking where he was from. We moved though topics about his home state before broaching the topic of God. Any conversation can be steered to spiritual things. Items relating to Christianity such as a book, bible, church bulletin, or tract can be handy for conversations. Conversations about movies or current events can all be steered towards God. I once talked to a waitress about a hamburger and the conversation lead to talking about God. Remember, God created everything, Jesus walked in the flesh, and the Church is active in all parts of the world; therefore, you can arrive at the subject of God from any topic.

It is important to guide the conversation. This doesn't require any special training or knowledge, just keeping your mind on the task at hand. If you are focused on where the conversation is going, and keeping the goal in mind, you will get there. It's easiest to make the transition from random topics to Christ with a simple question like, "What are you doing this weekend?" You can then share your plans about church and ask if they attend church. People can be open to sharing what they believe, especially about the church. Many don't go and will quickly give you a reason. Others are fringe members, and will give excuses. Be sure to listen. Asking questions is more than just leading a conversation. Listening to what is said will give you clues to the personality and type of person that is before you.

Consider these entry points you may have missed:

- Talking about church

- Talking about religion

- Items in the news

- Special events or holidays with a religious theme

- Tragedy or life-changing event

- Questions or misconceptions

▢   Movies or TV shows

Entry points are easy to find or create. Explore tactics such as bringing along Christian music or magazines when traveling. Use your surroundings to raise Christian issues. Listen to a Christian radio station. A Christian t-shirt, bumper sticker, or accessory can be an entry point. Use things you have, and always look for items you can use to begin conversations about Jesus. Sometimes you will need to create an encounter. Open the door and make arrangements. Plan and prepare.

Use your tools to initiate the conversation, allow the person to ask questions, and explain the item and its value or use. Do not use judgmental or condescending language or condemn the person for their choice of music or fashion. A change will only occur once a person is born again, and a non-Christian will not have Christian values.

The quickest way to end an evangelistic contact is to be insincere. If you ignore the person or fail to listen, you will not be heard. Listening is very important. Try to discern the keys that formed their beliefs. Comments that arise about Christian items like music or books can be a clue about their hang-ups. Many people get ideas and visions of God from family or experiences. Some of them have been hurt and have a negative opinion of God and the church. It takes time to build trust with one who has been hurt. Someone who claimed to be a Christian has often offended Skeptics or Opposers, and you will have to work though those issues. Some will tell you about praying to receive Jesus as Savior, and then rejecting Him. Don't be shocked. Remember that Jesus said many will say to Him "Lord, Lord". Jesus said in Matthew 7:23 that He will answer, "I never knew you". Listen and give some truth, always in love, never by force or though degradation. Arguments will not help a person who is hurt receive the grace and love of Jesus Christ. Letting the issues go without talking through them will not help a person receive grace. It's a balancing act, but it's worth the effort. The most positive thing you can do as a believer is help people break the stereotypical view they hold of Christians.

It may be helpful to do some basic study on Biblical Counseling. I am not recommending that everyone need to get a degree, or take hours of classes to share the gospel, but a book on this subject may prove helpful. If you come upon a situation like this, and have no counseling experience, don't worry. The important thing to remember is, you know the answer to the big problem, and that is the person of Jesus Christ. Listen and provide truth and clarity to issues and problems about God and Jesus Christ. He open, be honest, and be caring without making any judgment.

Take time to listen, and to care; if something arises that you can't handle, do not be afraid to get others involved. If you suspect abuse of any kind, try to get that person help as soon as you can. In some states, if you find a case of child abuse, you are required to report it. Seek help from a pastor or Christian counselor you trust and work though these situations. Don't be afraid or intimidated. Most people just need someone to listen and care about them. Anything beyond this, it may be helpful to refer the person to a pastor or counselor. Discover the resources available and be ready to ask for help from those qualified to give it.

Entry points will help you assess the situation, and open the door to share more. An entry point can last for a few minutes or a few years. Always remember to ask questions, listen, and guide the conversation. In time your relationship will grow, and you will have more opportunities to share the gospel. Moving someone toward the point where they are ready to hear and receive the Gospel may take a great deal of time in prayer to establish. Remember, above all things, pray.

Questions to ask yourself:

What entry points can I create?

What entry points already exist?

How will I plan to control and steer the conversation?

What resources do I have to help me if I need them?

Where do I go for help?

Openness

As you begin sharing with people, they will open to the gospel. We are told in II Corinthians 4:10 that we have the power to destroy strongholds. These strongholds are often what is keeping people from comprehending the truth of the Gospel. As we pray, share, build relationships, and connect with people, we will see strongholds begin to fall. Sometimes it happens rapidly, but often it takes time. The strongholds can be seen as their openness to the gospel, and I have found 5 levels or stages. Each stage presents you with an opportunity to share different parts of your testimony, and each has its own challenges.

-Stage one. The first stage of openness is defined by an unwillingness to listen to what you have to share. Many "Not Quiters" are at stage one due to past experiences. They don't want to know about Jesus and they don't want to talk about church, often because of a negative or hurtful experience. This stage is often the most difficult because you never want to force your beliefs on anyone. They must make a commitment to Christ, but they can't do this by compulsion. Begin by asking questions and try to work through the issues that have them closed.

At this stage, there isn't much you can share without being invited. Asking questions and developing a relationship will slowly open the door to sharing. You must keep in contact with the person, and moving from this stage may take a great deal of time. Demonstrate love and compassion in tangible ways. You may be the first Christian who has ever cared about them, so don't give up. Pray for them, and let them know it. Ask others to pray for this person, and ask the Holy Spirit for guidance. Although this stage may take time to get through, don't be surprised if you move through it quickly. Love and compassion can tear down walls so quickly that you may find they are moving beyond this stage quicker than you anticipated. Remember, everyone with whom you share is different; no one will move through this or any other stage in the same way or at the same rate.

-Stage two. During this stage, the person with whom you are sharing is more willing to listen, but will not give much consideration. This is a good time to share your testimony while continuing to ask questions. You may find many Outsiders and "Not Quiters" at this stage. If you find yourself sharing at this stage, take your time. Find ways to maintain contact every day. It may take several points of contact before you make any progress. Ask questions and share truths that will help the person think and open up. Expand on dialogue whenever possible and allow the person to contribute as much as they are willing to the conversation. It's like building a bridge over a river; it takes planning and time. Be receptive to their opinions and pose questions about what they believe. Often they have beliefs they have never examined and questions may help open the door. Engage in dialogue instead of merely giving information. They will probably be hesitant at first, but continue to ask and encourage. Continue praying and talking with others about your progress.

-Stage three. At stage three, there is more willingness to dialogue. You will find many Skeptics and Opposing Views at this stage. Dialogue may be open, but often it will be in the form of arguments and "what if" questions. Be patient. Part of this process may be an attempt to test you to see if you are genuine. Once they discover you are not a superficial or judgmental person, they will open up more.

Apologetics will be useful at this stage. 'Apologetic' means giving an explanation for something. When using Christian Apologetics, you are giving the reasoning and evidence for your belief in Jesus. Apologetics will not save anyone, but it may help dispel some misconceptions. Only faith in Jesus can lead someone to salvation. Knowledge will not get them into Heaven, but it may open a door to accept Christ. You may be required to study some cult beliefs to answer questions. You may encounter individuals who have had success in frustrating Christians, and may have a series of questions they love to ask. There are many resources to answer questions about the claims of Christ, the Bible, the Church and other issues. Check out The Case for Christ by Lee Strobel or Evidence that Demands a Verdict by Josh McDowell. Check with your church for other resources to answer hard questions.

When encountering an argument, remember you are not trying to win an argument. No one really wins an argument. Your role is answering questions and presenting the truth. Above all, respect and love. Answering questions and showing genuine concern will do more than winning an argument. This can be the most difficult stage, and many Christians shy away from sharing when confronting this stage. It's not necessary to have the answers to every question. No one does. Don't be overwhelmed if you find yourself stumped by a question, or at a loss for words. Some questions they present don't matter, and don't be afraid to say "that doesn't really have anything to do with what we are talking about." If you respect their opinion and are willing to listen, they will respect you.

At this stage, many questions are asked for the purpose of stumping you or presenting a roadblock. Often at stage three, you will hear a question like "if God is good, why are kids starving in Africa?" This is a valid question, but the reality is, most don't lose any sleep over kids starving in Africa. We should, but we don't. People who are dead in sin don't really care about starving kids in Africa; they care about themselves. People are mainly focused on the here and now. Answer the question the best you can, realizing they don't really want or care for an answer. There is no "right" answer to this question. Your role is communicating truth, you won't convince them with a solid argument. Keep the relationship open, warm, and friendly. Remember, above all things, pray.

-Stage four. Stage four is much like stage three, but the questions are increasingly valid. These people will reveal purpose and curiosity instead of arguments. Many Outsiders may jump to this stage quickly, seeking for answers to their questions. Questions about sin, Jesus, or other religions may come up. It will be helpful to know some apologetics, but most questions can be answered directly from the Bible. At this stage, they no longer wonder about kids in Africa; they want to know why they suffer or why someone they love is having a hard time. Remember to be patient. Don't be afraid to share the gospel more than once in different ways during this stage. A person must understand sin and the punishment for sin. Talk about Jesus and why He died. Keep your presentations simple. We will explore how to present the gospel in later chapters.

This is an exciting stage in which to be, for there is often a great deal of open dialogue. Keep going at their pace; don't try to force the issue before they are ready to accept. The Holy Spirit may be working on them, so ask the Spirit to guide you as you proceed. No one can come to Jesus unless God calls them (John 6:44). Remember to keep praying.

-Stage five. This is the stage in which the person is open and ready to accept the gospel. You will occasionally encounter a seeker who is already at stage five, but most of the time you must work toward this stage. In this stage you can ask if they have ever accepted Jesus as Lord and Savior. Your focus at this stage should be communicating how to become a Christian and what it means. This stage is the most rewarding of all, but continue working until the job is completed. Share the Good News and remember that even after the person prays to accept Christ, the need assistance getting involved in a local church and Bible study. When someone prays to accept Christ, it's not the end of the journey, but the beginning. Continue to pray, and rejoice with the angels.

I cannot stress enough that moving through the stages can be a slow process that takes hours, days, weeks, months, or even years. Moving though these stages can also happen very quickly, as quickly as a few minutes. God can take a closed heart and open it to the gospel before your eyes. You may find yourself with some back-up from another believer entering the conversation. God will equip you in many ways. Be open to the Spirit, be flexible, and let God work in the situation. It will change their heart and yours.

Consider the factor of time. If you know this is a situation that you do not have time to develop, such as on an airplane, you may feel led to proceed to the gospel presentation regardless of the stages. It is very important to share the Gospel with those you will only see once, and there are ways to share quickly. This is the most difficult type of evangelism. You will not know this person well, and you may be nervous. Remember to pray and ask for help. You never know when God will bring you into a situation to share with someone you'll never see again. You may never know the impact, but it might be God using you to change the world. You may be the right person at the right place at the right time We will discuss in later chapters the ways to present the gospel, and many of these would work just fine in these situations. In most situations, be deliberate, pay attention, and remember to begin and end everything with prayer.

Making it Work

Once you have discovered the type of an evangelist that fits you, what type of person you are sharing with, and the stages of openness, you can make a plan to share your faith. Let's explore how. For reference, see Appendix C.

Remember, they will be an Opposer, Skeptic, "Not-quiter", Outsider or Seeker.

Now that you know who you are and the initial level of receptivity of the other person, consider what stage category they fit into. Do they listen when you talk about God? Do they seem open to talk about spiritual things? Do you know their church background or religious beliefs? Asking yourself some quick questions should help you to identify which stage they are in and the best way to proceed.

The first thing you must do is find a place and time to share with this person. Do you see them at work, at school, or some other location? Plan a time to share that will be open and free of constraints. If you can, plan for a recurring time so you can continue the conversation over an extended period of time. Remember not to share in a time you are supposed to be doing something else. Sharing the Gospel is the most important thing you can ever do, but it's not a good example to be irresponsible with your duties or responsibilities. Find a time that is free. It won't be much help if you can't share with a person because you got fired, so plan appropriately.

Now, to walk through the stages. Let's use the example of a Passive evangelist who we will call Chris. Chris is sharing with an Outsider we will call Allison. Chris and Allison are both in college and see each other in the student union before class. They have known one another for years, but never really talked about church. Chris will begin with Appendix A and go over the Do and Don't Do list. He will find passive and follow the column down to outsider and read over the information. Chris finds that he needs to ask questions, share the basics, and share his testimony. Chris remembers from experience what he sees in the do not section. Previously, he had stopped sharing before reaching the invitation. Chris remembers sharing the gospel, but never asking if the person wanted to pray to receive Christ. There have also been times when he backed down and let someone justify their sin. After looking through Appendix A, Chris plans to see Allison on Monday between classes. They will both have an hour to talk. Using Appendix B, Chris reviews some outlines (we will discuss outlines later) and knows who to contact for help.

He has also informed those he asked to pray of the time and place he will share with Allison, and he knows they are praying for him.

Chris is a little nervous as he sits down, but soon begins to chat about the class. The conversation moves to the previous weekend, and Chris relates a little about his church experiences on Sunday. He and Allison begin some small talk about church. She shares that she is Catholic but rarely attends mass. She is quiet about what she believes, but Chris asks open-ended questions and makes pleasant conversation. As they talk, Chris considers the best way to discuss sin and communicate lostness. He listens for clues that indicate whether religion or someone at church has hurt Allison. Their dialogue comes to an end and it's time to go to class. By the end of the conversation, Allison began opening up and asking basic questions, such as the difference between Protestants and Catholics.

Chris tells Allison he would like to talk more, and she agrees. He has left the door open to share more in the future, and Allison will be thinking about God until they talk again.

This example is completely fictional, and there are millions of possibilities for how a conversation can proceed. Take one step at a time, and make notes at the end of your conversation to be sure you continue making progress. Rely on God and the Spirit's promptings as you move through the process. Remember, with everything you know and learn, your relationship with God and compassion for the lost are the most important tools you possess.

Your Story

Once you have entered into dialogue with a person, it's important to share your testimony. This serves two functions; to share what God has done for you, and building a stronger friendship by sharing experiences. Testimonies come is all shapes and varieties. The most common testimony that you will share is your Salvation Testimony, but there are also prayer and church testimonies. Each will help you share truth.

Salvation Testimony. All Christians have a story about when they started a personal relationship with Jesus. It happens at all ages, and everyone has a different experience. You can find the Apostle Paul's testimony in Acts 26. In this chapter, Paul tells of his conversion to Herod Agrippa. It falls nealy into three parts: his behavior before conversion, his conversion on the road to Damascus, and his lifestyle afterward.

Your testimony should have three similar parts. People may argue with the Bible, but they cannot argue against the evidence in your life. They may argue that the change doesn't happen to everyone, as with people who claim to have prayed for salvation, but didn't accept Christ. You can be encouraged that truly giving your heart and life to Jesus Christ will bring a change. Share that Jesus changed your life, and He can change everyone's life. Remember to keep your testimony simple and include the most important aspects. They do not need to know your entire life story, only how God has changed and rewritten it through His saving grace. Try writing out your testimony and practicing it. It shouldn't take more than a few minutes to share.

What were you like before you became a Christian?

What happened in your life to lead you to the Gospel?

Who helped you?

What do you remember about the experience?

How is your life different?

A Prayer Testimony is also helpful when sharing with Skeptics or Opposers. A time in your life when you reached up to God for help and He answered you in a supernatural way is always a great story to open dialogue. You will find that your testimony will peak some curiosity and cause the person you are sharing with to think. All humans are selfish by nature, and they will be interested in hearing the Gospel to discover what is in it for them. Never share the Gospel by sharing selfish gain, but you can use the curiosity of gain to open dialogue. Jesus spoke frequently about rewards. There are blessings that result from following Jesus. It's acceptable to speak of the blessings, but be careful not to share a false gospel that is all about getting what you want.

Revealing some of your own needs and struggles will help lower defenses and open lines of communication. This demonstrates the evidence of God's love in your life, and allows you to share God's love for the person. Be sure you don't present God as a genie in a bottle, but as a living, loving Lord with whom we have a relationship.

A Church Testimony is helpful for Outsiders and "Not Quiters". These individuals need to see church as more than a group of hypocrites that sing boring songs and preach at each other. Sharing the support and love of other Christians may be a foreign concept to people who do not receive much love from friends or family. Sharing how your church has helped and supported you may give them the opportunity to see the Church as something other than what they have believed.

Bringing someone to church with you makes sharing the Gospel much easier. They are in a situation and mindset that is more receptive if they are in an accepting group of believers. Use some caution, however. If you bring a lost person to church where they are shunned, rejected, or judged, it will me much harder the share the Gospel. Don't lie about your church, and if you church has some unspoken rules, be sure that people will feel comfortable. If everyone in your church wears a suit and tie, don't tell your friend to come in jeans and a t-shirt. They will feel awkward. If all their worst fears about church are confirmed on their first visit to your church, they will not make a second visit. Make sure you paint a realistic picture of your church while sharing your church testimony. You want to show them a picture of the body of Christ, not an amusement park.

Sharing testimonies will bring the message of Jesus to life. As you share, remember that you are sharing an exciting and life-changing event. Make it personal, keep it short, and include the important parts. Remember with whom you are sharing and their personality and life experiences. Different aspects of your testimony may be emphasized for some, but not for others. People are different, so the presentation of your testimony should be varied for different people.

Communicating Lostness

Lostness is the foundation of communicating the gospel. No one will ever be found until they realize they are lost. Salvation comes as a response to brokenness. Sharing lostness can be the most difficult or the easiest part of the presentation. Many will have no problem admitting they are sinners. Many will cling firmly to the belief that they are good people and deserve to go to Heaven. There are many, many factors that will vary in every situation. The belief that everyone must find their own unique way to Heaven will lead a person away from accepting lostness. The belief that there is no God will also lead a person away from accepting lostness. The concept, however, is one that must be understood to move to a gospel presentation.

Lostness is summed up in one word: sin. The nature of God is in direct opposition to sin. God and sin do not mix. God does not allow sin into Heaven. No exceptions, no debate. All sin must be atoned for, and the wages of sin is death. The bible is clear that blood must be shed in order to obtain forgiveness. And not just any blood; only sinless blood will suffice. "The wages of sin is death" (Romans 6:23). Someone must die to atone for your sin before the holy court of God's justice: you or a substitute. And the only substitute without personal sin to atone for is Jesus Christ. Without this understanding, the reality of hell and our own depravity will never be accepted. We must understand our condition; we are separated from God because we are sinful and rebellious. Sin is more than simply doing bad things. We are rebellious at the core and have turned away from and abandoned God.

There are several important things to remember when communicating lostness. Each person must take ownership of their sin. Be sure you utilize suitable examples. When talking with children, ask questions such as "Have you ever hurt your brothers or sisters, or disobeyed your parents?" With older students you may ask, "Have you ever broken the rules, or acted rudely?" There are a few 'safe bet' questions such as "Have you ever told a lie?" No one need confess their sin to you, but they must understand they have sinned and their sin must be dealt with. Help them understand that sin is in our nature, and they are powerless against their sin.

When discussing lostness, never use guilt or appear judgmental. Remember that you, too, have sinned and fallen short of God's glory. You have the same problems as those with whom you are sharing. The only difference is Jesus set you free and they are still in bondage. Conviction of sin is the work of the Holy Spirit. Give guidance and support but never condemnation. You cannot free someone from the prison and bondage of sin by making them feel bad.

Many will reject the concept of lostness because it depends on the premise of absolute truth. This issue has been debated for centuries, and there are many ways and resources to equip you for debate. You will probably never meet anyone who believes in complete ethical relativism. Ethical relativism is the assertion that there is no right or wrong, no binding moral laws, that you do what feels right and what is right to you. Absolute relativism means I could do whatever I wanted with no legal restraints. I have yet to meet someone who believes it is acceptable to be violated, so relativism is not practical.

You can overcome the issue of moral relativism vs. absolute truth by the example of someone making an offense against another person. Such actions are not only possible, they happen regularly. One can also offend God, and that is sin. Regardless of how society or culture feels about an action or attitude, if God declares it to be sin, it's sin. God decides who is going to Heaven or Hell, based upon His moral judgments that have been violated, so His opinion is the one that matters. If a person doesn't believe in God, you have a long way to go to convince them of lostness. It's important to demonstrate that God has a standard, and it's this standard that we have all missed. By sharing from this point, we can explain lostness without casting judgment or condemnation.

Remember not to use church words or terms. Words or phrases like sin, salvation, justification, sanctification, or 'born again' will only confuse. Be clear when explaining what it means to be lost. Think back to when you were first told about sin. Try to put yourself in their shoes, and answer all the questions you would have in similar circumstances.

Speak in such a way that it would be clear to you if you were still without grace. The bondage of sin is strong, and the only way it will be overcome is by the Holy Spirit. Your role is to share the nature and cause of sin, the consequential separation from God, and the resulting judgment against us because of disobedience. The Holy Spirit is the only one who can bring true repentance. He will work through you, so be faithful. Use scripture when you can and, of course, remember to pray.

-The Good News

Sharing the Good News of Jesus Christ is the goal. It is the point toward which everything thus far has been aimed. This is very exciting, but frightening or even overwhelming as well. Take everything a step at a time. Don't rush or become nervous. If you have an outline, stick to it and don't try to change things to fit a situation. If you try to make each part relevant to a particular person, everything becomes confused. Be clear and relaxed. Sharing the Gospel is universal, and Scripture has power. Just share what the Bible teaches.

Getting to this point can be a long process or a quick conversation, depending on how well you know the person and how well they know you. If they know you are a believer or attend church, it may be different than sharing with a co-worker who knows little about you. No matter the situation, approach everyone the same and simply share the truth in love. Ask yourself, "Where am I in my relationship with this person?" Use that common ground to share truth.

Some situations will not allow time to develop a relationship. Perhaps you are at a bus stop or airport, in an airplane or on a business trip, and you will never see this person again. Maybe you are in restaurant or other public place and, although you may see this person again, it will be impossible to forge a continuing relationship. In these situations, you should make every attempt to share the gospel. Each of the previous stages can be rushed, by asking questions and quickly guiding the conversation. Ask questions to the point, such as "Do you believe in Heaven?" This may cause you to break some of the previous rules. You may need to guide the conversation more and provide less time for questions. Asking questions that go straight to the heart of the matter are best. Then simply share Biblical truth.

It may be impossible to go through the stages of openness. Sharing with someone not open to the gospel will seldom yield fruit, but it is important to share. You never know what God is doing in a person's heart, so present the gospel in a clear manner, using a good deal of scripture.

If the situation is conducive to continued contact, it's acceptable to share the gospel frequently and throughout various stages. Research demonstrates that it takes an average of 7 to 10 gospel presentations before someone will accept. The Holy Spirit will use your words and break down strongholds. He will work in the person, so be faithful. Don't push the issue, simply share the truth. Feel free to wait for doors to open, and add variety to the presentation. If you find yourself using the same verses or outline every time, find a new presentation. Avoid becoming redundant; you will be ignored. Keep it fresh. Try different approaches and contexts.

In the next section we will explore outlines for sharing the gospel. Make these outlines your own, learn them, and vary them. Memorization has its place, and knowing an outline or presentation by heart it a great tool. However, everyone with whom you share will be different. Take ownership of your presentations, then you can be prepared to adjust them. You should know three strategies for sharing: a visual strategy, an auditory strategy, and a hands-on strategy.

-A visual strategy is something that you can show people. It's often a picture or drawing. Having something you can jot down and show will help those who learn visually. Visual aids are helpful in sharing, and having a focal object can enhance clarity. In addition, it relieves the pressure of being in a busy environment with attention-grabbing distractions. If you can draw a simple illustration on a napkin or piece of paper, the hearer can take for later reference. A picture helps many people connect the dots.

-An auditory strategy is the most common, and is simply a strategy shared though spoken conversation. It does not require any other materials, and can be shared anywhere. These strategies will be the backbone of your gospel presentation, and will make up the bulk of what you share. Scripture teaches, "So then faith comes from hearing, that is, hearing the Good News about Christ" (Romans 10:17). Telling people about Jesus will be part of every strategy. You should learn a variety of ways to tell people about Jesus, and make them your own. Use scripture often; there is power in God's Word.

-A hands-on strategy requires getting a person involved. There are tools the hearer can use themselves, as well as plans that involve handing the person a Bible, tract, or other book that they use to walk though the Gospel. This strategy requires foresight and materials, but is often fruitful, especially with young people. Some biblical concepts are difficult to understand, and holding a visual aid will add clarity. Any time you can get a Bible into someone's hand and help them read it, that is great progress.

Elements of each type should be incorporated into your presentation as often as possible. Remember, everyone learns differently, and understanding the Gospel message is a form of learning. Becoming a Christian will change a person like nothing else, so be sure they learn the lesson well. Make a habit of carrying the materials you need, such as a small Bible, pencil and paper, tracts, or other tools. As you utilize different strategies, outlines, and objects, you will become comfortable using them.

Many great tools are available at your Christian retailer, online, and in your own imagination. There are tracks, tools, toys, and even sports equipment with gospel imprints. There is a resource for almost any situation, so find one that fits you, the setting, and with whom you want to share.

-Outlines and Strategies

There is no shortage of programs and outlines to share the Gospel, so always look into new and different ways to share your faith. Some methods will be presented in this material, but don't limit yourself to just this book. Learn as many programs, outlines, and strategies as possible. The more you learn, the more principles you will find, and the easier it will be to personalize your own strategy.

Some of the greatest materials ever written are in your local Christian bookstore. Share Jesus Without Fear by William Faye is a great tool to know and learn. The Evangicube is a wonderful hands-on tool available in Christian bookstores or at www.evangicube.org. Check out The Mission Ball at http://themissionball.org/ for a great sports outreach. Programs such as FAITH, The Net and others are available to learn and use. There are numerous conferences on sharing. Ministries such as Campus Crusade for Christ and Fellowship of Christian Athletes have materials and workshops. Obtain and use these materials if possible; discover the principles that are universal. Websites such as www.thekristo.com are great multimedia resources. Tracts are available from your local Christian Bookstore. Check with your pastor for resources available at your church.

All strategies have basically the same process of sharing truth and asking for a response. They may vary in the questions asked, verses used, or manner of communication, but they are all basically the same. Many will use the same key verses and the same illustrations. These tools all focus on the same goal: sharing that Jesus is the Savior, and asking if a person is ready to commit their lives to Christ.

Since we have already communicated lostness, the gospel presentation is a focus on salvation, but it's often helpful to go over the fundamentals of lostness again. Sometimes it helps to look at lostness from different angles. It's easy to emphasize global lostness when we see the fallen state of the world on the evening news. War, crime, and violence all attest to the wickedness of the fallen world. When speaking about the fallen world, it's simple to focus on our choices. We have all chosen sin, and now we are slaves to sin. It's important to highlight the choices we make, that we chose to disobey God and it's our responsibility. We choose to sin, and we must choose Christ as the only remedy. The Holy Spirit works in the heart of the person to show the sinfulness of our choices. Mankind made bad choices, and so have we.

Another route to the topic of lostness is the fall of mankind through Adam and Eve. They chose to sin by eating the fruit and, from that day, everyone has followed their lead. This is a great springboard to dialogue about Jesus because it is the biblical foundation of our need for a savior. It highlights lostness and it gets us to open the Bible and share from God's word.

Review this story in Genesis 3.

Include key verses when discussing lostness. Romans 3:23 declares that all have sinned. Romans 6:23 proclaims the wages of sin is death. Psalms 14:1-3 announces that there is no one righteous and all have turned away from God. Use these verses combined with questions such as, "Have you ever done anything you were ashamed of?" or "Have you ever broken any rules or laws?" Beware of asking vague questions like "Have you ever done anything wrong?" The word "wrong" is open to interpretation. Breaking rules is more concrete.

Becoming a Christian is more than saying "Yes, I've been bad". For someone to receive Christ, they must be convicted of sins, and you cannot do that. Only the Spirit can do that. You are working with the Spirit to produce conviction of sin. Never condemn or use guilt or coercion. True conviction only comes from the Holy Spirit. Until a person experiences conviction, they will never seek repentance.

From Lostness, we must focus on hope. Share that there is hope, a way to come back to God. They know that all sin must be punished, and you can share that shedding blood brought forgiveness of sin. Hebrews 9:22 explains that without blood there is no forgiveness. The Good News of the Gospel is that Jesus died and shed blood to forgive all sins. Because Jesus is perfect, He can forgive all sin. To obtain forgiveness, we must ask and place our faith in Him.

We can be forgiven by asking Jesus to forgive our sins, and committing to follow Him. Avoid difficult words unless there is opportunity to explain them. Repent means to turn away from something and toward something else. Sin is violating God's standard of right and wrong.

Share the verses that communicate how to receive Christ:

- Romans 10:9, "If you confess with your mouth that Jesus is Lord and believe in your heart that God raised him from the dead, you will be saved."

- John 14:6, "I am the way, the truth, and the life. No one can come to the Father except through me."

- Revelation 3:20, "Look! I stand at the door and knock. If you hear my voice and open the door, I will come in, and we will share a meal together as friends."

- Romans 10:13 is important: "Everyone who calls on the name of the LORD will be saved."

By sharing this way, many arguments about other ways to Heaven are avoided. We have all sinned, and sin must be dealt with. Sin is only atoned by shedding blood. No other religion or church has a god or leader who died to forgive sin, therefore Jesus stands alone. He alone bore the cross and died for us. One of my favorite verses is Romans 5:8: "But God showed his great love for us by sending Christ to die for us while we were still sinners."

A visual illustration such as The Bridge is often helpful. It can be drawn in parts to show the separation of God and man through sin, and the cross the bridges us to God.

There are other that can be drawn on a board or sheet of paper. Visuals are helpful if you find it difficult expressing ideas through words alone. With computers and the Internet, the possibilities are endless.

Sharing the Gospel in a variety of ways is an important skill. Some people learn best by hearing, some through sight, and some need hands-on for the most effective learning. There are plenty of studies and research on learning and learning styles. Since we can't do learning assessments on everyone we share with, it's important to try all the learning styles. If you recognize that something works better than everything else, center on that style, but attempt to include all styles as much as possible. There is no real connection between the types of lostness and a learning style. A seeker, an opposer, or a skeptic can be any learning style. This is why relationships are so important. As you understand a person better, your communication will improve. That is why we must love people the way Jesus does.

Gospel plans that use a schedule that can be very helpful. The EXIT Strategy by the North American Mission Board is a four-to-eight week cycle with four parts. Each part focuses on something different and ends with a celebration where lost friends are invited and explained the Gospel. FiSH by Campus Revolution is a similar strategy that works in a group. It is an intentional program combining many aspects to reach your friends. They present each piece in a clear way that can be very helpful in leading others to Christ.

Learning an evangelism strategy in never a waste of time. Be intentional, take time to learn, and develop your personal strategy. Begin by finding a strategy that works for you. Find one that is adaptable for sharing with those with whom you spend the most amount of time. Attend training, go to conferences, visit websites, and read books. The more you know, the more tools you will have to use and choose from.

At this point in my life, I spend most of my time with students. I work with the college group, and with high school students, especially while substitute teaching. It is important for me to be able to share in a way that is non-confrontational, especially in a public school setting. I have found it easiest to have a prop with me to introduce the subject, such as a book or Bible. I can begin dialogue using these aids, and move to a key question. "Would you like to know what Christianity is really about?" This secures permission to share some facts educationally, and not "promote religion". I can share from the beginning about sin and the fall of mankind with Adam and Eve. Then I can talk about Jesus, and present the Good News. It gets tricky asking a student to pray and accept Christ, but you can generally discern when a student is open and can proceed.

In some situations, at work or in a public school setting, you must proceed with care. I would encourage you to invite someone to accept the Gospel as often as possible. Make it personal and keep the goal before you. Take your time and make the most of the tools you possess. Share as much as you can, even if you don't have time to finish; God can still use your obedience to reach the lost world.

-Your Invitation

Inviting someone to accept the Gospel of Jesus Christ is the point that everything else is focused upon. It's the moment of truth, and may by the part about which you are the most anxious. When asking someone to accept Christ, you may be rejected. It is important to move beyond the fear of rejection to ask the question. The question can take different forms:

- "Do you want forgiveness from your sins?"

- "Would you like to accept Jesus as your Savior?"

- "Would you like to give your life to Jesus?"

The form of the question can be different, but there are some truths you must be sure you include in your invitation.

Accepting Jesus is a personal choice. You don't become a Christian because you go to church, because your parents are Christians, or because you were baptized as a baby. One becomes a Christian by putting faith in Jesus Christ and inviting Him to take control of your life. We each bear the responsibility to respond in faith, so as we talk to people about Christ, we must invite them to respond. The Holy Spirit will work in and through us to draw people; we need but do what we have been called to do.

Becoming a Christian is life-changing. The Bible tells us that we are new creatures in Christ. Things will begin to change in the life of a new believer. Make sure you don't present the Gospel as the solution to the hardships of life. The life of a Christian is often more difficult that being lost. The world and Satan are now enemies of the new believer, and things will be difficult. The power of the Holy Spirit makes it possible to overcome, and the joy of the Lord is present in the life of the believer. All these changes will become evident to the new believer as they walk in faith and obedience.

These things will not occur without an authentic relationship, entered into by asking Jesus to be Lord and Savior and turning from sin. This will be clear after a complete Gospel presentation, and if the person understands lostness, they will be in a position to understand grace. Explain the Gospel clearly, but never assume someone understands what it really means to be born again. If a person doesn't understand they are separated from God, they cannot seek to be united with Him.

When inviting someone to accept Christ, press for a definite 'yes' or 'no' answer. This is the only way to eliminate all misconceptions. The person may have questions. They might inquire about lifestyle choices, current relationships, or similar issues. Be clear and honestly address their concerns. If you receive a cryptic answer, such as "I want to accept, but I'm not ready yet", probe a little deeper. Ask what prevents them from accepting. Often you will get an "I don't know" answer. Encourage the opportunity of the moment, that there is no better time than the present, but do not to push. They may need time to let things process, so don't end the conversation too quickly.

If they say "no" then the invitation is over. There is no need to continue with an invitation. We will discuss in the next section how to use encouragement. If the Holy Spirit is not working, and if the heart is not open, you cannot force it. Continue to share and pray and be open. Ask if you can continue to pray for them. Keep the relationship alive in order to talk about things again. There may be things going on in their heart, and the Holy Spirit may be working. Keep praying and looking for opportunities to share the truth. Keep the lines of communication open, and keep the relationship active.

-Praying Together

Once your friend answers affirmatively regarding their willingness to accept Christ, it's time to guide them in prayer. The concept of "praying to receive Christ" is not in the Bible, but there are solid Biblical reasons for what we do. First, it follows the admonitions of Romans 10:9, providing a seeker the opportunity to confess faith in Christ with their mouth. Second, teaching a person to pray and seek God is the first lesson of discipleship. Prayer is important because it helps the new believer begin on the right foot by getting accustomed to the lifeline of prayer. Leading a prayer with another person may seem an overwhelming concept, but it's really simple. As believers, we should have a habit of praying each day during our quiet time. Praying with other believers is a powerful thing, and if you are not in the habit of praying with people, I encourage you to find someone to pray with on a regular basis.

Be aware that the person you are about to pray with has never truly prayed before this moment. They may have "gone through the motions" of praying, but without a relationship with Jesus as Lord and Savior, those prayers never made it past the ceiling. It would be like talking on a phone with no connection. Talk all you want, but there is no one on the line. This is the first prayer of a new believer, so you will model praying for them. Keep is simple and never use religious talk. For example, words like "thee" and "thou" are not more sacred or holy; they are simply old. These words are no longer part of modern language; they are only used in some churches and at Renaissance festivals. If you are not sharing with someone dressed in full armor, I suggest not using Old English. Keep it simple.

Here are some guidelines:

Begin with a simple address to God. I would suggest starting with the name of Jesus, since you are asking Him to come into this person's heart. Addressing a prayer to Jesus will keep the focus on Jesus.

Next there must be confession of sin. Keep Romans 10:9 in mind: "Confess with your mouth Jesus as Lord." First confess the sinful nature and resulting sinful choices, then confess Jesus as Lord.

Pray about belief. Belief never results from words, but we must reinforce important truths such as, "I believe you died and rose from the grave, and I believe you save me from my sins." This prayer comes from the heart, but it also helps the person understand the commitment they are making. Sometimes a person becomes overwhelmed with emotion and brokenness, and this process helps them to focus on the decision at hand.

The last thing to pray is a commitment. Tell Jesus that He is now the Lord and Master, invite Him in, and give Him complete control. Conclude the prayer in the name of Jesus.

Here is a model prayer. You do not have to use this model every time, but try to use each element in the prayer.

Dear Jesus, I am a sinner and I know I need forgiveness for my sin. I ask you to be the Lord and Master of my life. You are Lord, and I believe that you died and rose from the grave to save me from my sins. I commit my life to you. In the name of Jesus I pray, Amen.

-Discipleship

Once a person accepts Jesus as their Lord and Savior, the next step is the process of discipleship. The Great Commission instructs us to "make disciples of all the nations, baptizing them in the name of the Father and the Son and the Holy Spirit. Teach these new disciples to obey all the commands I have given you..." (Matthew 28:19-20). Our task is not finished until there is a mature disciple. We must not neglect shepherding, caring for, and encouraging our new Christian brother or sister. We must be sure they are in a place they can connect, grow and be supported.

It is essential to connect them to a local church and a small group. The best way is to bring them to church with you. In this way you can introduce them to friends, teachers, and mentors, as well as guide them through the next steps in their newfound faith. Talk with them about baptism, and explain its importance regarding obedience. It is a public confession and something we do to identify ourselves as being newly united with Christ and desiring to be more like Him. Jesus tells us if we confess Him before men, He will confess us before the Father (Matthew 10:32). Baptism is how we confess in many churches, and it identifies us as Christians. Sitting down with your pastor and the new believer is often helpful in sharing the reasons for being baptized, and scheduling a date. There are many materials available to help you talk about baptism, discipleship, and other issues that may arise.

When an invitation at your church is given, go forward with the new believer, and stand with them, pray with them, and support them. Introduce the new believer to your friends and church family. No one is ashamed of a new baby when it is born into the family, so make sure you introduce your new brother or sister in Christ. We are saved into the family of God, and no infant can survive left on its own. Help your new brother or sister in Christ to get into a place of acceptance and growth. Help them connect with other believers and become part of God's family. Mentor and guide them as they grow in their new faith.

Connect the new believer into a small group Bible study. Maybe there is a study you teach or maybe it's just the two of you. If your church has a New Believer's class, encourage them to attend. Pray that God will open doors and hearts and the new believer will develop relationships with the people of your church. It was a relationship that helped you lead them to Christ, so relationships will be key to helping them grow in Christ.

There will be questions to answer and skills to teach. The new believer must be taught how to pray, study the Bible, and of course, share their faith. Share what you know, and help where you can. Find discipleship classes and resources to help the young Christian grow. The Survival Kit for New Christians is a great resource or the New Christian's Handbook by Max Anders. If your church teaches this as part of discipleship training, encourage the new believer to attend, or get the materials and take them through it. This is the critical time to build the foundation of faith. Most importantly, take time to invest in the new believer. We are called to make disciples, so your job is not over. Walk with them as they grow until they in turn make disciples.

There will be times that you cannot personally help in the process of discipleship. Those were situations in which you shared and never saw the person again. In these instances, be proactive. Try to get an address and ask permission to ask a church to contact the person. Try to stay in communication, and send them a Survival Kit for New Christians or other resource in the mail. When you can, carry resources to give away to people who accept the Good News. Find a tract, or write a note to encourage those you might come in contact with. Do whatever you can to get new believers connected with a Church and discipleship. You wouldn't leave a baby alone to fend for itself; the same is true with new believers.

What If They Say No?

The hardest thing to hear when you ask someone if they want to pray to accept Christ is "no". This can be heartbreaking, especially if you are sharing with a family member or friend. If you share your faith with someone who you thought was receptive or open to the Gospel, but they say no, it's hard. What do you do? What do you say? How do you handle the situation?

Every evangelist or evangelism strategy will tell you not to feel rejected; the person didn't reject you, they rejected Jesus. I have told myself this many times, and it still hurts. To know that someone has just rejected the thing in which I have spent my life devoted to requires more than just thick skin. When someone turns away from the one thing that will give them eternal life, it hurts. It's hard, and it's okay to be a little upset. When we have found truth and someone rejects the truth, we struggle, and it can cause doubt. I believe you would be calloused not to grieve a little for this individual who has just rejected the most wonderful gift in all of eternity.

It is okay to grieve, but you must remember it's not permission to give up on evangelism or on the person. Sharing may become more complicated after a "no", because now you must share without offense. Presenting a straightforward outline will be less and less effective. So, what is the best way to proceed?

Immediately after the rejection, don't close down, even when it's your first reaction. Encourage the person and ask why they don't want to accept. It may be a misconception; they may believe they have to sell everything they have and live in a cave. Try to help them move though their hesitation if it is based on fasle assumptions. Be sensitive, let them know you care, and that you are curious as to why they would reject Christ. If they are unsure, encourage them to think about it. Encourage them to ask God to show them the truth. Offer to help them study the Bible. Show care and concern without guilt. If the person gets defensive, that is your clue to back off. The Spirit may be working, and the timing is just not right.

As you encounter the person and maintain the relationship, continue to encourage them. Invite them to church or other activities once in a while. If you can plan a non-threatening event that other believers will attend, that may be helpful. Chat about Christian topics and ask their opinion about things. Spend time and continue to cultivate the relationship. Continue to pray and over time you may see The Holy Spirit open their heart.

There are some sobering things to remember. Jesus himself said that more people will follow the wide path to destruction than the narrow gate that leads to Heaven (Matthew 7:13). It may be our desire to have everyone come to know the Lord, but it's not going to happen. Some people will die rejecting Jesus. Your role is to make sure they have the chance to hear the Good News. How sad it will be to see all those we failed by never giving them a chance to accept Jesus as Lord and Savior. You cannot soften a heart that is hardened, but you can pray that it will become soft.

Seek out those who have accepted Christ after a struggle and rejection. Ask them what caused their change of heart. They may give you insight on how to proceed next. Look for those who can walk beside you and help you understand in order to share more effectively. Most importantly, remember to keep praying.

Thinking About It

Sharing the Gospel of Jesus is something that we are all called to do. It is an overwhelming task to be transformed into a Great Commission Christian, but we have all the tools and resources we need to make the journey. It is my hope that you will find help in this book to share your faith again and again. Be sure to make copies of the worksheets in the back of this book for everyone you are sharing with. These tools can be used over and over again to focus on sharing with friends and loved ones. Thinking through the process and your procedures will help you get more confident.

In evangelism, you will encounter spiritual warfare. We have an enemy, and he doesn't want the gospel to spread. Many Christians have been caught in the devil's snare and have not shared the Gospel. The most effective weapon you have is prayer, so pray often and pray with others. Ask others to pray for you and meet with a group for prayer and support. Think about the people who can pray for you and when you can meet for prayer. Do not neglect this crucial aspect.

My prayers are with you as you walk through your everyday life and look for opportunities to share. I pray that God will bring you someone today with whom you may share the love of His Son. I pray we can all make a difference in the social circles in which we live, work, and play each and every day. God has positioned you in a unique place to do His work, and He has great blessings. We just need to plan and go.

Appendix A

	Active	Passive	Not Me
Opposer	Do: Listen, share, emphasize, encourage, ask questions, offer opinion. Do Not: Argue, belittle, mock or ridicule, use negative body language, raise your voice.	Do: Listen, discuss, dialogue, ask questions, share opinions. Do Not: give up, clam up, let them control the conversation, compromise or give in.	Do: be active, dialogue, ask questions, share opinions. Do Not: Shy away, give in, give yes and no answers, give up or give in.
Skeptic	Do: Share, be open and honest, encourage, ask questions, offer your opinion, share knowledge, try to understand, study and learn. Do Not: Tease, belittle, argue, become defensive, intimidate or strong-arm.	Do: Listen, emphasis, encourage, ask questions, share beliefs, try to understand, study and learn. Do Not: Let them control the conversation, compromise, agree to disagree, give in or give up.	Do: Listen and ask questions, share your beliefs and opinions, learn what you can, share what you know, admit when you don't know. Do Not: Be intimidated, shy away from questions, lie your way out of questions.
Not-Quiter	Do: Encourage, support, emphasis, ask questions, dialogue open. Do Not: Dominate the conversation, belittle, use guilt, argue or get frustrated.	Do: Share personal testimony, give support and encouragement, listen and dialogue. Ask questions. Do Not: Let them get away with excuses, shy away from hard questions.	Do: Share personal experience and give support, ask questions and listen and dialogue. Do Not: Shy away, let them control the conversation, clam up.
Outsider	Do: Share the basics, talk openly, ask questions, listen and be honest. Do Not: Ridicule, use guilt or fear, dominate and overwhelm the entire conversation, use Christian buzz words.	Do: Ask questions, share basics, be clear, share your testimony. Do Not: Quit before you share and invite them to receive the gospel, allow them to justify sin.	Do: Be honest, share truth, be clear, share your testimony. Do Not: Let the conversations die out, let them dominate the conversation, shy away from sharing and inviting.
Seeker	Do: Go though entire Gospel, ask and make sure they understand. Do Not: Rush the presentation, leave them without support after they are saved.	Do: Be clear and share the entire gospel, use and give material and support, follow up. Do Not: Use vague language, give them material without follow up, rush through.	Do: Share and invite, be clear and give them helps to continue to grow. Invite them to meet your pastor or attend Sunday School. Do Not: Shy away from sharing, give them material without follow up, let them try to find it on their own.

Appendix B

Where I go for help:

My Church's office number is: _____

Others who can help with follow up (example, Sunday School teachers, missionaries, others pastors, deacons).

Name	Phone Number

My Evangelism Outlines are:

_____

_____

_____

My evangelism accountability partners are

Name	Phone Number or E-mail

Other People I will ask to pray for me.

Appendix C

Worksheet

I am a _____ evangelist. I am sharing with a _____.

I will share at (location): _____. At what time (lunch, break, etc): _____

_____

Stages (Begin at the appropriate stage):

Stage one: Find entry point. Begin talking and building relationships. Ask questions to find background and beliefs.

Begin thinking about:

What outline might I use?
How will I communicate Lostness?

Stage Two: Use entry point to continue to share. Find new ways to start conversations about God. Continue to ask questions and find out about background, beliefs and misconceptions.

What is there belief system?
What is keeping them from Christ?

Planning

Which outline will you use?

_____

How will you communicate Lostness?

Stage Three: Clear up questions and misconceptions, avoid arguments and share personal testimony. Share bits of the Gospel and begin to talk about Lostness. Show love and respect.

Who will you have praying?

Stage Four: Answer questions, help to find the truth. Give practical helps from your life experience, like sharing a prayer testimony. Begin to share parts of the Gospel and continue to talk about Lostness.

Stage five: Share the truth. Choose the outline you will use and share the gospel and Invitation. Be sure you are prepared for follow up.

Appendix D

Information Sheet

My friend is (fill in name)_____

They are a (circle one) **opposer   skeptic   not-quiter   outsider   seeker**

There stage of openness is _____

What I know about their church background: _____

_____

Questions they have: _____

_____

Notes and things to remember: _____

_____

_____

_____

www.ingramcontent.com/pod-product-compliance
Lightning Source LLC
Chambersburg PA
CBHW081228040426
42445CB00016B/1915